Marlene Sway, Ph.D.

Bats

Mammals that Fly

Franklin Watts - A Division of Grolier Publishing
New York • London • Hong Kong • Sydney • Danbury, Connecticut

For my husband, Dean Ramus

I would like to thank Sara van Dyck and Joanne Sala for their generous help with this manuscript. Special thanks to Elana Kraft for her suggestions and to Paul Weir for his constant encouragement and support.

Photographs ©: Animals Animals: 35 (William Gray); Art Resource: 40 (Erich Lessing); Bat Conservation International, Inc.: 42, 43 bottom (Karen Marks); ENP Images: 5, 31 (Michael Durham), 6 (Gerry Ellis), cover, 16, 17 (H.C. Kappel/BBC-NHU); Merlin D. Tuttle: 1, 12, 13, 29, 33; Photo Researchers: 37 (Stephen Dalton), 23 (Gregory G. Dimijian), 4 top (Jerry L. Ferrara), 39 (Michael McCoy), 25 (Tom McHugh), 4 bottom, 21, 27, 41 bottom, 43 top, 7 (Merlin D. Tuttle/Bat Conservation International), 15; Photofest: 41 top (Geordie Johnson); Visuals Unlimited: 19 (Bruce S. Cushing).

Illustrations by Jose Gonzales and Steve Savage

Visit Franklin Watts on the Internet at:
http://publishing.grolier.com

Library of Congress Cataloging-in-Publication Data

Sway, Marlene, 1950–
    Bats: mammals that fly / Marlene Sway.
    p. cm. — (Animals in order)
    Includes bibliographical references and index.
    Summary: Provides a general overview of bats, including descriptions of fourteen species, information about why many people fear them, and a discussion of efforts to preserve bat populations.
    ISBN 0-531-11449-X (lib.bdg.)   0-531-15943-4 (pbk.)
    1. Bats—Juvenile literature. [1. Bats. 2. Endangered species.] I. Title. II. Series.
QL737.C5S95   1999
599.4—dc21   98-2704
                                                                          CIP
                                                                          AC

GROLIER
PUBLISHING

Contents

Not a Bird, Not a Mouse

You're playing outside as it gets dark. You look up at the evening sky and notice the jerky flight of "birds" above you. You wonder why

they haven't returned to their nests yet? Actually, most birds have returned to their evening perches. Those flitting creatures in the sky aren't birds— they're bats. How can you tell the difference between a bird and a

Bald eagle

Fisherman bat

4

House mouse　　　　　　　　　　　　　　　　　**Keen's bat**

bat? It isn't always easy, especially from a distance. If you saw a bat close-up, though, you'd realize that birds and bats are very different.

Some people think bats look like mice with wings. That's because most bats have small and furry bodies, like mice. But a bat isn't even a close relative of a mouse. In fact, you are just as closely related to a bat as a mouse is.

Look at the pictures above and those on page 4. You will see that even though bats are not closely related to birds or mice, they do share some important features with these other animals.

Round leaf horseshoe bats

Traits of a Bat

Both bats and birds have wings. If you look carefully at a bat's wings, you will see that they are really hands with long, bony fingers and even a thumb covered by a thin layer of skin. A bird's wings are very different. They have a complex bone structure and are covered with feathers.

Most bats are active at night. During the day, they sleep, hanging upside down in caves or other dark places. Because bats hunt when it is dark, many use a kind of natural radar called *echolocation* to find food. As a bat flies through the air, it makes a series of high-pitched calls. When the sound hits a fluttering insect or a swimming fish, it bounces back toward the bat. By listening to the echoes of its calls, the bat can pinpoint the exact location of its *prey*.

Many bats get the energy they need to stay alive all winter from fat they store up during the summer. In the late fall, they look for a quiet place, such as a cave or an abandoned mine, to spend the winter. As they hang motionless, their body temperature falls and their heart rate slows down.

In colder climates, most bats *hibernate*. They spend a long period of time at rest. In warmer places, like Mexico and Egypt, bats go into *torpor*—a much shorter resting period. Between each resting period, the bats are active. Some bats migrate during the coldest months of the year. They fly to warmer areas where there is plenty of food.

Most female bats have one baby, or *pup*, each year. Pregnant females search for a protected roosting area, such as a cave or a barn. Often, hundreds of females roost and raise their young together. Baby bats drink mother's milk until they are old enough to digest solid food. When the baby bat learns to fly, the mother and pup cruise the night sky together.

A mother bat with her pup

The Order of Living Things

A tiger has more in common with a house cat than with a daisy. A beetle is more like a butterfly than a jellyfish. Scientists arrange living things into groups based on how they look and how they act. A tiger and a house cat belong to the same group, but a daisy belongs to a different group.

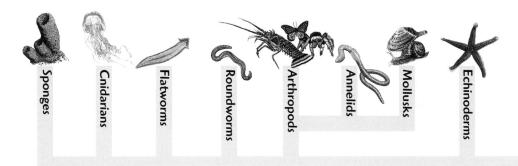

Sponges   Cnidarians   Flatworms   Roundworms   Arthropods   Annelids   Mollusks   Echinoderms

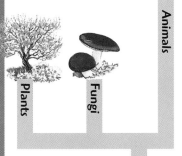

Plants   Fungi   Animals   Protists   Monerans

All living things can be placed in one of five groups called *kingdoms*: the plant kingdom, the animal kingdom, the fungus kingdom, the moneran kingdom, or the protist kingdom. You can probably name many of the creatures in the plant and animal kingdoms. The fungus kingdom includes mushrooms, yeasts, and molds. The moneran and protist kingdoms contain thousands of living things that are too small to see without a microscope.

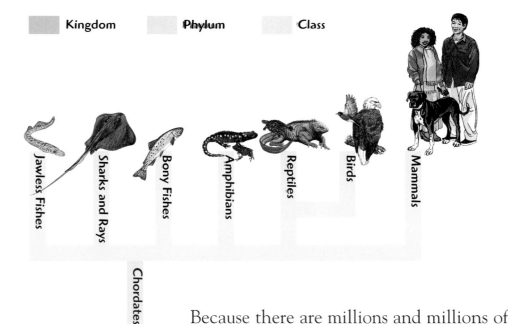

Kingdom · Phylum · Class

Jawless Fishes · Sharks and Rays · Bony Fishes · Amphibians · Reptiles · Birds · Mammals

Chordates

Because there are millions and millions of living things on Earth, some of the members of one kingdom may not seem all that similar. The animal kingdom includes creatures as different as tarantulas and trout, jellyfish and jaguars, salamanders and sparrows, elephants and earthworms.

To show that an elephant is more like a jaguar than an earthworm, scientists further separate the creatures in each kingdom into more specific groups. The animal kingdom can be divided into nine *phyla*. Humans belong to the chordate phylum. Almost all chordates have a backbone.

Each phylum can be subdivided into many *classes*. Humans, mice, and elephants all belong to the mammal class. Each class can be further divided into *orders*; orders into *families*, families into *genera*, and genera into *species*. All the members of a species are very similar.

9

How Bats Fit In

You can probably guess that bats belong to the animal kingdom. They have much more in common with sparrows and snakes than with maple trees and morning glories.

Bats belong to the chordate phylum. Almost all the chordates have a backbone and a skeleton. Examples include fish, snakes, owls, bears, and mice. Can you think of other chordates?

The chordate phylum can be divided into a number of classes. Bats belong to the mammals class. Elephants, humans, dogs, and cats, are all mammals.

There are seventeen different orders of mammals. The bats make up one of these orders. As you learned earlier, many bats have furry bodies and flexible wings supported by long finger bones.

Bats can be divided into a number of different families and genera. There are more than 1,000 species of bats. They live in every *habitat* on Earth except the Arctic Circle and Antarctica. You will learn more about these fascinating creatures in this book.

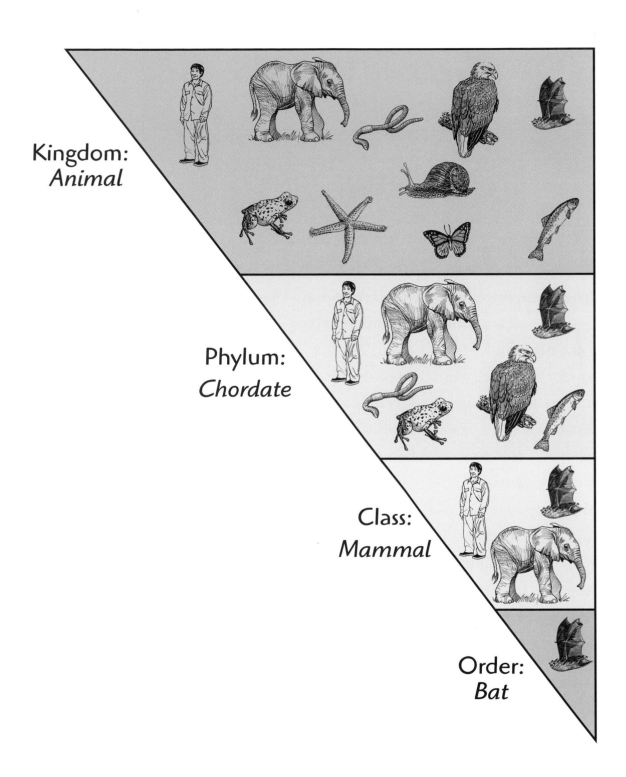

Kingdom: *Animal*

Phylum: *Chordate*

Class: *Mammal*

Order: *Bat*

Brown Bats

FAMILY: Vespertilionidae
COMMON EXAMPLE: Big brown bat
GENUS AND SPECIES: *Eptesicus fuscus*
SIZE: 1 1/4 to 3 inches (35 to 75 mm)

If you live in North America and have seen a bat, chances are it was a big brown bat. These bats live closer to people than any other American bat.

At one time, big brown bats lived in forests, but as towns and cities grew, these bats began setting up house in all sorts of places—bridges, tunnels, attics, bell towers, and even window shutters.

Big brown bats use echolocation to find and capture insects. Believe it or not, one of these bats can eat as many as 600 mosquitoes in just 1 hour. Big brown bats also help us by feeding on many of the insects that destroy our crops.

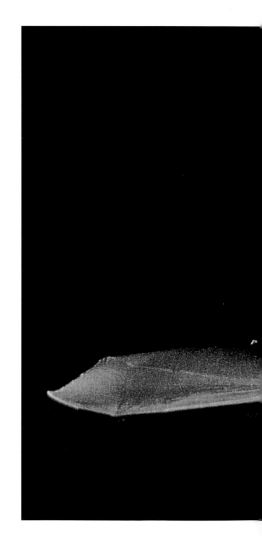

In the late summer, big brown bats begin to gain weight. They will use their stored up fat during the long, cold winter. From early December to late April, big brown bats hibernate in caves, or sometimes in old mines. In spring, the bats fly out of their winter homes and look for a place to spend the summer.

Free-tailed Bats

FAMILY: *Molossidae*
COMMON EXAMPLE: Mexican free-tailed bat
GENUS AND SPECIES: *Tadarida brasiliensis*
SIZE: 1 3/4 to 2 1/2 inches (44 to 64 mm)

The long, narrow wings of Mexican free-tailed bats are designed for high-speed flight. Their short, velvety fur doesn't slow them down a bit. Even the shape of their ears helps them lift off. They can fly 60 miles (97 km) an hour and reach a height of 10,000 feet (3,050 m).

These super-fliers live in huge groups. Every year, as many as 20 million bat mothers set up *nurseries* for their pups in Carlsbad Caverns in New Mexico and in Bracken Cave in Texas. When night falls, the mothers fly out in search of food. As a group, they can eat up to 250 tons of flying insects in a single night.

When the sun begins to rise, the bat mothers return to the cave. A bat mother has no trouble finding her own baby. She identifies her pup by its scent and its peeping call. Bat babies are just as skilled at finding their mothers.

In late summer, Mexican free-tailed bats migrate to areas with warmer temperatures. Some travel up to 900 miles (1,450 km) to caves in Mexico and then go into torpor. When spring arrives, the bats return to their summer homes in the southwestern United States.

15

Long-eared Bats

FAMILY: Vespertilionidae
COMMON NAME: Long-eared bat
GENUS AND SPECIES: *Plecotus rafinesquii*
SIZE: 1 3/4 to 2 3/4 inches (45 to 70 mm)

My, what big ears you have! That might be the first thing you would say to a long-eared bat. This bat's ears are almost half as long as its entire body. Its huge ears help the long-eared bat hunt for food and avoid danger.

When a long-eared bat searches for a meal, it throws its ears forward to pick up insect sounds. If it detects an insect while flying, the bat grabs its prey in midair. If the insect sounds are coming from the ground, the long-eared bat hovers near the insect like a hummingbird and then scoops it up.

When this bat hears the sound of an enemy, it hides in rock crevices. After a few moments, the bat sticks its ears up to see if the danger is gone. If the *predator* is no longer nearby, the bat climbs out of its hiding place—ears first.

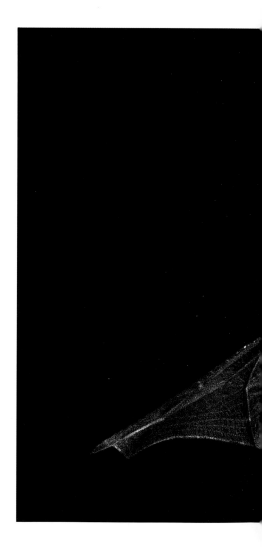

Long-eared bats can be found in deserts and pine forests. They roost in rock crevices underground for most of the year. But in late spring, the females set up *maternity colonies* in large, old trees. Long-eared bat mothers usually choose trees that are between 150 and 300 years old. When the young bats are old enough to fly, they begin to hunt for themselves.

Fisherman Bats

FAMILY: Noctilionidae
COMMON NAME: Fisherman bat
GENUS AND SPECIES: *Noctilio leporinus*
SIZE: 3 3/4 to 5 inches (98 to 132 mm)

It's close to midnight. Tourists are fishing off the coast of Costa Rica. Suddenly, they see something falling from the sky. Their guide tells them not to panic. What they have just seen is a fisherman bat hunting for its dinner.

The orange fisherman bat has face like a bulldog, and strong hind feet. It also has sharp claws, which the bat uses to catch thirty to forty fish each night.

Like other bats, the fisherman uses echolocation to locate prey in freshwater and saltwater environments. When the bat spots a fish, it swoops down into the water and grabs the fish with its huge clawed feet. The fisherman bat often bites its prey into small pieces and stores them in its cheek pouches. Later, the bat flies to a safe spot and enjoys its fish dinner.

Fiherman bats usually roost in sea caves, rock crevices, or holes in trees. It's not hard for scientists to locate their roosts. All they have to do is sniff until something smells fishy.

Like ducks, fisherman bats have a glistening layer of oil on their wings. The oil repels water, so the bat's wings never get so wet that it

can't fly—even if the bat accidentally falls into the water. When this happens, the fisherman bat swims by using its wings as oars.

Frog-eating Bats

FAMILY: Phyllostomidae
COMMON NAME: Frog-eating bat
GENUS AND SPECIES: *Trachops cirrhosus*
SIZE: 3 to 3 1/2 inches (76 to 88 mm)

Can you name a bat that has a swordlike nose, warts on its lips, gigantic ears, and an appetite for frogs? The answer is—the frog-eating bat. This unusual-looking, cinnamon-colored bat is found in humid, lowland forests from southern Mexico to southern Brazil and on the island of Trinidad in the Caribbean. It usually roosts in caves or abandoned railroad tunnels. In Trinidad, it roosts in holes in trees.

Frog-eating bats pluck their prey off plants or the ground. Unlike other bats, frog-eaters don't rely on echolocation to find food. Instead, they use their supersensitive hearing. When frogs croak out love songs during their mating season, these bats pick up the sound and fly directly to them. When they can't find any frogs to eat, frog-eating bats feeds on lizards, insects, or fruit.

The frog-eating bat's big ears work like an *antenna*—they make the frogs' sounds louder. When one of these bats hears a croaking frog, its brain goes right to work. It knows whether the sound is coming from a frog that would make a good meal or a frog that is poisonous.

Tent-building Bats

FAMILY: Phyllostomidae
COMMON NAME: Tent-building bat
GENUS AND SPECIES: *Uroderma bilobatum*
SIZE: 2 1/4 to 3 inches (54 to 74 mm)

If you're ever in Mexico, Bolivia, or Brazil and think you see a skunk camping out in a tree, don't worry. It's really a tent-building bat. This shy little creature is grayish-brown with white stripes running down its nose and back. Its nose looks like a horseshoe with a small spear sticking out of it.

Tent-builders live up to their name. These bats bite through palm leaves to create a home with a fan-shaped roof. Once the roof is in place, the bat uses its very sharp teeth to make footholds on the tree trunk, so it is easier to climb in and out of the tent. As many as forty bats can live in one of their custom-made tents.

A tent-building bat's favorite food is fruit. But if it can't find any, it will eat pollen, *nectar*, or insects.

Vampire Bats

FAMILY: Phyllostomidae
COMMON EXAMPLE: Common vampire bat
GENUS AND SPECIES: *Demodus rotundus*
SIZE: 2 3/4 to 3 1/2 inches (70 to 90 mm)

There are about 1,000 different kinds of bats on Earth, but only three are true vampires. These bats, which need to drink fresh blood to survive, live in Central and South America.

Vampire bats feed only on sleeping animals. And, in most cases, the animals never know that the bat has sucked some of their blood. The common vampire bat gets most of its blood from cows, but it also preys on horses and donkeys. These bats almost never bother people. But, once in a while, they feed on a person who is sleeping outdoors or in an open shack.

The common vampire bat leaves its daytime roost every evening. It flies just above the ground, and uses its incredible hearing to detect the rhythmic breathing of snoring animals. When the vampire finds the snoring prey, it tiptoes around the animal several times to make sure it is really asleep. Then the bat licks a spot on the animal's ear or neck. A substance in the bat's *saliva* makes the animal's blood flow more easily. Next, the vampire bites off a circular piece of the animal's skin and spits it out. Finally, the bat presses its lips against the wound, so that its lower lip and tongue form a pipe. Over the next 30 minutes, the bat sucks out about 8 teaspoons (39 ml) of blood.

Mouse-tailed Bats

FAMILY: Rhinopomatidae
COMMON NAME: Mouse-tailed bat
GENUS AND SPECIES: *Rhinopoma microphyllum*
SIZE: 2 to 3 1/2 inches (53 to 90 mm)

If you ever have a chance to visit ancient Egyptian pyramids, you will find tombs and mummies of great pharaohs and their queens. You'll also get a good look at all kinds of ancient splendid royal treasures. You may also see bats. Don't be surprised, bats have been hanging out with mummies for more than 3,000 years.

The mouse-tailed bat is a strange little creature. It looks like a mouse with a very long tail. It has huge ears, a sunken forehead, and a "nose leaf" that can curl over its nostrils to block out dust and sand. This unusual feature comes in very handy because mouse-tailed bats usually live in deserts.

During the winter, the weather grows cooler and the insects that mouse-tailed bats like best are hard to find. Inside the quiet pyramids, mouse-tailed bats go into torpor. During this time, the bat hunts, drinks water, and moves around much less than it does during the rest of the year. It lives off a layer of fat stored under its skin.

Fruit Bats

FAMILY: Pteropodidae
COMMON NAME: Hammer-headed fruit bat
GENUS AND SPECIES: *Hypsignathus monstrosus*
SIZE: 7 1/2 to 12 inches (193 to 304 mm)

Hammer-headed fruit bats are found in the African countries of Gambia, Ethiopia, and Angola. They live in forests, near swamps and rivers. Most of the time they roost in mangrove and palm trees. Their favorite food is fruit, but hammer-heads will eat birds and chickens, too.

If you ever see a male hammer-headed fruit bat, you'll know how this bat got its name. It looks like a little flying camel with a square snout and huge nostrils. Large air sacs inside its nose and throat help the male bat attract mates. As air passes through these sacs and over its large voice box, the bat makes a loud, honking call. Female hammer-heads find this sound irresistible.

Female hammer-heads are more delicate and graceful than the males. Their faces look like a tiny dog's face. Hammer-heads mate twice a year. Between June and August, the males gather in one area. They fly to the tops of the trees and begin to honk away. Just imagine how noisy 100 honking bats must be! You might find all that noise annoying, but as far as female bats are concerned, it is music to their ears. About 6 months later—from December to February—the bats repeat their mating ritual.

28

Epauletted Bats

FAMILY: Pteropodidae

COMMON EXAMPLE: Wahlberg's epauletted
   fruit bat

GENUS AND SPECIES: *Epomophorus wahlbergi*

SIZE: 5 1/4 to 7 inches (135 to 180 mm)

Have you ever seen a bat in a military uniform? You'll see plenty of them if you go to central Africa. Epauletted bats look like they're wearing a brown or gray uniform with white furry patches, called epaulettes, on the shoulders.

These epaulettes have an important purpose. Most of the time, male epauletted bats hide their patches in pouches on their shoulders. These pouches have glands that give off a strong odor. While the epaulettes are inside the pouches, they soak up this scent.

During the mating season, male epauletted bats pull their patches out of the pouches. Whenever a female bat cruises by, the male beats his wings so that his scent fills the air. At the same time, he calls out with a high-pitched honking. Female epaulatted bats are very attracted to this behavior.

Epauletted bats live in fields or forests. They like ripe fruit and fruit juices. Their specially shaped throat is perfect for sucking juices out of their favorite fruits.

False Vampire Bats

FAMILY: Megadermatidae
COMMON EXAMPLE: Yellow-winged bat
GENUS AND SPECIES: *Lavia frons*
SIZE: 2 1/2 to 5 1/2 inches (65 to 140 mm)

The yellow-winged bat has been called the prettiest bat in the world. It has long, fluffy blue-gray or blue-brown fur and yellow wings and ears. This bat also has huge ears and an unusual nose.

Unlike other bats, yellow-wings mate for life—every male bat has young with only one female. When a baby bat is born, each parent has a special job to do. The father guards the area and chases away intruders. When the young bat is hungry, its father returns to the roost and stays with the baby while the mother hunts for food. The parents follow this routine until the bat pup is old enough to catch its own insects.

Most yellow-winged bats live in fields or wooded areas near a lake, river, or swamp. They like to roost in acacia trees because this tree's flowers attract the insects the bats enjoy. Most of the time, yellow-wings hang upside down from a branch and wait patiently for an insect to fly by. When the bat spots a potential meal, it swoops down, catches the prey, and then returns to the tree to eat its meal.

Naked Bats

FAMILY: Molossidae
COMMON NAME: Naked bat
GENUS AND SPECIES: *Cheiromeles torquatus*
SIZE: 4 1/2 to 5 3/4 inches (115 to 145 mm)

There's no reason to blush if you see a naked bat. It's perfectly normal for it to walk around with no hair. This unusual-looking bat is about the same size as a newborn piglet, and it looks like one, too. The naked bat's thick, elastic skin is usually black or dark brown. These bats are fairly common in Southeast Asia. They spend most nights cruising above wooded areas and rice paddies in search of insects.

When a naked bat roosts, it tucks its wings into special skin pouches. With its wings out of the way, it is easy for a bat to use its four little feet to climb to a comfortable spot inside the tree hollow where it lives.

Every naked bat has a large throat sac filled with glands. This sac, which is covered with black bristles, is filled with a strong-smelling liquid. Scientists think the bat uses this liquid to mark its *territory*, so other bats stay away during the mating season.

A naked bat mother almost always gives birth to twins. After dining on mother's milk for a while, the young bats learn to catch termites and other insects for themselves.

Flying Foxes

FAMILY: Pteropodidae
COMMON EXAMPLE: Indian fruit bat
GENUS AND SPECIES: *Pteropus giganteus*
SIZE: 3 3/4 to 7 inches (95 to 177 mm)

On the island of Tonga, people tell an ancient story about a beautiful Samoan princess who gave their king a pair of flying foxes as a gift of love. The Tongan king liked these doglike bats very much. He decided to make flying foxes and their babies royal property.

Flying foxes have velvety, grayish-brown or black fur with yellow or grayish-yellow fur between their shoulders or on their necks. Unlike most bats, flying foxes are often active during the day. Large groups of these bats often roost in a single tree.

The roof of a flying fox's mouth has eight bony ridges that help the bat get its favorite food—the juices of tropical fruits. When a flying fox bites into a mango or a fig, it presses the fruit against these ridges with its tongue. Squeezing the fruit releases the juice.

After it drinks all the juice from a piece of fruit, the flying fox spits out the pulp and seeds. If the seeds land in fertile soil, they grow into a new tree that will produce more fruit for the bats to eat.

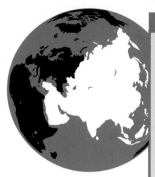

Blossom Bats

FAMILY: Pteropodidae
COMMON NAME: Blossom bat
GENUS AND SPECIES: *Macroglossus lagochilus*
SIZE: 2 to 3 inches (50 to 72 mm)

Sometimes people mistake the blossom bat for a butterfly. This delicate, reddish-brown bat lives in wooded areas of the South Pacific islands.

The blossom bat has a long, thin tongue covered with tubelike bristles. When it sticks its tongue into a flower, the bristles go into action. They work like straws, so that the bat can suck up nectar. While the bat feeds, the flower's powdery *pollen* sticks to the bat's furry face. So when the blossom bat moves to another flower, the pollen from the first blossom falls into the next one. The blossom bat doesn't realize it, but it is helping the flowers produce new seeds.

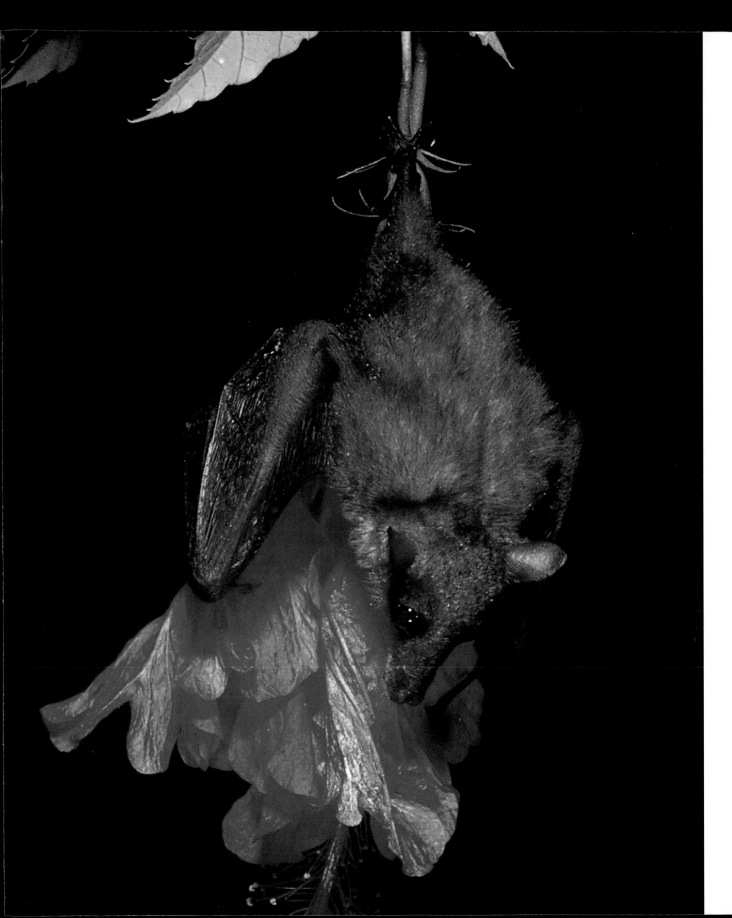

As the story was told and retold, people added new details. Some said Dracula could turn into a bat or transform other people into vampires. Others said vampires could be repelled with garlic or be killed with a stake through the heart.

The Count Dracula legend has caused people in Europe, North America, and South America to fear bats, but in other parts of the world, many people like bats. In Asia, for example, people believe that bats bring good luck. A Chinese design shows five bats flying in a circle. This design is a symbol of continuous good luck and happiness.

As you can see, bats don't really deserve their bad reputation. Recently, people have begun to understand all the ways bats help us. Some carry pollen from one plant to another. This helps plants create new seeds. Other bats scatter the seeds. The plants that grow from these seeds are often stronger and healthier than plants that grow alongside their parents. Still other bats eat mosquitoes and insects that feed on our crops.

Today, people realize how important it is to protect bats and their habitats. In the 1970s, the gray bat became the first bat listed as an endangered species in the United States. Six types of bats are now considered endangered in America, and government officials may soon add eighteen others to the endangered species list.

One of the people who has worked hardest to protect bats is a scientist named Merlin Tuttle. In 1982, he formed an organization called Bat Conservation International. This group's national headquarters is in Austin, Texas—a city known as the "Bat Capital of

Bats leaving their roosting spot under a bridge in Austin, Texas

42